Suzy
the Hungry Gull

Charlotte Lindquist
Illustrated by Cindy Klund

Suzy the Hungry Gull
This story will transport you to the shores of Lake Superior in Minnesota.

Here is where you will meet Suzy the herring gull, and she will tell you the story of her hunger and how her brothers saved her life.

The characters are fictional. The information written about herring gulls is factual and is printed in blue.

The themes running through this story are hunger, sibling love and loyalty, and survival.

ISBN: 978-0-57870-518-7

Published by Book Baby

Dedication

One in five young children in the United States are going hungry.
This book is dedicated to all the children in our country that are struggling with hunger.
Ten percent of all sales of _Suzy the Hungry Gull_ will go to Feed My Starving Children.
FMSC is a non-profit organization that provides nutritious meals to hungry children around the world.

There is no such thing as a seagull!

My name is Suzy.
I am a herring gull.
Did you notice I did not say seagull?

There are approximately 50 species of
gulls found throughout the world. There
is not a single species called the seagull.

During my first year of life, I had many bad days because I was hungry.
Many nights I had a hard time falling asleep because I was hungry.
Many mornings my stomach hurt because I was hungry.

Young herring gulls have spotty brown feathers and a black beak.

Here is my story.

My life started in the springtime in a nest built on a rocky cliff along the lake.
The rocky cliff protected the nest from the strong winds.

The nest was made of twigs and dead grasses.

My mother even lined the nest with feathers, so it was nice and soft.

After the nest was built, my mother
laid a clutch of three eggs.

**A clutch of eggs is the total number
of eggs laid in the nest at one time.**

She laid two eggs on Monday and one
egg on Tuesday.

The first and second eggs laid were my
two brothers Burtt and Buzz.

The third egg was me.

Mom and Dad each took turns sitting on and turning the three eggs.
They would each sit on the nest for about five hours at a time.
This process is called incubation.

After about three weeks our eggs hatched.

My brothers' eggs hatched on Saturday.

I hatched on Sunday.

All three of us hatched with our eyes open.

We were covered with a fluffy layer of fine, soft feathers called down.

The third egg to be hatched in a herring gull clutch has a hard time getting enough to eat. Because I was born a day later, I was smaller, weaker, and grew more slowly.

Burtt and Buzz were bigger and pushed me aside at eating time.

When Mom and Dad were four years old a red dot appeared on their beaks.
When we were hungry, we would peck at the red dot.
Mom and Dad would then regurgitate (throw up) the food into our mouths.

It took us about six weeks to **fledge**.
This meant we had grown enough large feathers
on our wings so that we could fly.

I had enough feathers to fly.
But I was not strong enough to fly.
Burtt and Buzz always got all of the food.
I never got enough to eat to grow strong.

Burtt and Buzz flew off to explore the lake.
Will I ever see them again?

After Burtt and Buzz flew away I was the only one being fed by Mom and Dad.
I was lonely but I was not hungry.
For six weeks I cried at them and pecked away at the red dots on their beaks.
Every time I was hungry, I got food to eat.
Soon I was strong enough to fly away too.

When young herring gulls are able to fly and search for food on their own, their mother and father leave them.

Now I had to find my own food!

I loved flying.
I loved gliding through the air.

After a day of flying, I got so tired that I could not fly anymore.
All I could see below me was the lake.
I remembered Mom telling me that my feathers are waterproof.
I landed on the water and fell asleep.

Luckily herring gulls can sleep on calm lakes!

Gulls open and close their eyes while sleeping so they
can keep watch for any dangers around them.

In the morning, I realized I needed to look for something to eat.
I was so hungry after flying all day.

Mom and Dad were not there to feed me.
This was the first time I had to find my own food.

How would I do that?

I floated towards the shoreline.
I did see some fish that I was going to try to catch.

Just then, another hungry herring gull swooped
down   and fought with me
over the fish.

He got the fish!

Back to the shore I went.
I sat and rested.

That old familiar feeling of hunger was back.
I was starving.

I looked down and saw some flying ants crawling around on the sand.
I only got a few before they all flew away.

I was so hungry.
I had no energy.
I was so tired.

**I tucked my head under my
wing and took a nap.**

When I woke up I had just enough energy to fly to a campground to find a trash can.
While I was trying to dig out some food scraps to eat, I got string tangled
all around my feet.

I could not walk.
I could not fly.
I had to keep pecking at the string to chew it off my feet.

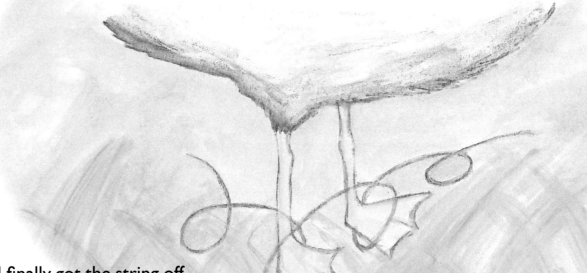

I finally got the string off.
That left me too tired to keep looking for food.
I left the campground still very hungry.
Herring gulls can only survive two days without food.

The evening brought very cold temperatures.

I was so cold I had to stand on one leg.
I pulled the other leg up against the
warmth of my body.

By standing this way,
I didn't lose as much
body heat through my legs.

That night, I was not only
hungry, but freezing cold!

Later that night there was a heavy rainstorm.

My feathers kept me from getting wet and helped keep me warm.

I sat very still to save energy.

Suddenly, there was a huge bird circling over me.

It was an eagle!

I remember Dad telling me that **eagles like to eat herring gulls!**

Meanwhile, Burtt and Buzz were enjoying life.
They lived in a **colony.**
A colony is a group of gulls living together.
They never had any problems finding food to eat because they lived near people.
Sometimes it made people very angry when they took their food off of the picnic table.

Burtt and Buzz were lucky that gulls are protected under the Migratory Bird Treaty Act. This act made it against the law to hunt, capture, or kill a gull.

Burtt and Buzz would steal food from the large fishing boats' picnic area.
They would swoop down, scaring people, and grab the picnic food in their
beaks and fly away with it.

A family was grilling a steak on the grill.

Buzz grabbed the steak
off the grill and flew away with it.

Burtt and Buzz would steal the fishermen's bait right out of his minnow bucket.

Minnows tasted so delicious.

The fishermen would yell and chase them away.

Lucky for me that **up until one year of age, young gulls still recognize each other.**

While Burtt and Buzz were flying around exploring the area, they spotted an eagle circling over a very weak herring gull.

When my brothers recognized that it was me, they chased the eagle away.
I had just enough strength left in me to lower my bobbing head and hold open my beak.
Burtt and Buzz knew that I was starving to death.

Burtt stayed to protect me and keep me safe.

Buzz immediately flew to the lake and brought back a fish for me to eat.

Burtt and Buzz fed me and kept me safe until I grew strong again.
They taught me that the easiest places to find food were where
people lived and ate.

We spent most of our days around
fishing shacks, campgrounds, fishing
boats, and picnic parks.

All three of us always
found plenty of food to eat.

Living with Burtt and Buzz made my days very happy.

I was never hungry again!

About the Author

Charlotte Lindquist is a teacher by profession. She has taught kindergarteners through fifth graders for 40 years. Her inspiration to write children's literature came about because she always found it challenging to discover books for her classroom that enabled the child to practice their reading skills, enjoy a fun story, and have a learning experience all at the same time.

She is using her teaching skills and years of experience to disguise learning in the most fun way though this book.

About the Illustrator

Cindy Klund is the daughter of the author. She is the artist whose talent tells this story with her amazing watercolor pencil images to compliment her mother's words.

Together they created a collaborative piece of art titled Suzy the Hungry Gull.